Ribich
pers.

D1257297

Crabapples

Big Cats

Bobbie Kalman & Tammy Everts

Crabtree Publishing Company

www.crabtreebooks.com

Crabapples

created by bobbie kalman

In memory of Jim Elder

Editor-in-Chief
Bobbie Kalman

Writing team
Bobbie Kalman
Tammy Everts

Managing editor
Lynda Hale

Editors
Petrina Gentile
Janine Schaub

Computer design
Lynda Hale
David Schimpky

Color separations and film
Dot 'n Line Image Inc.

Printer
Worzalla Publishing Company

Special thanks to
John Becker at the International Society for Endangered Cats

Illustrations
Barb Bedell: pages 9, 10, 11, 18-19, 20, 22, 29
Tammy Everts: page 13
Randy Rozena: page 27

Photographs
Nancy Adams/Tom Stack & Associates: page 13
Dominique Braud/Tom Stack & Associates: title page
W. Perry Conway/Tom Stack & Associates: page 23
B. Davis/Henry Doorly Zoo: page 22 (bottom)
Henry Doorly Zoo: pages 6 (bottom), 6-7
Diane Payton Majumdar: pages 28 (bottom), 29
Joe McDonald/Tom Stack & Associates: cover, pages 8, 12, 30
Gary Milburn/Tom Stack & Associates: page 25 (bottom right)
Kevin Schafer & Martha Hill/Tom Stack & Associates: pages 16-17
Dave Taylor: pages 7 (bottom), 10, 11, 14-15, 20, 21, 22 (top),
    25 (top, bottom left), 28 (top)
Robert Tymstra: page 24
Barbara von Hoffmann/Tom Stack & Associates: pages 4-5, 9, 26
Robert Winslow: page 17 (bottom)

Crabtree Publishing Company

PMB 16A
350 Fifth Avenue
Suite 3308
New York
N.Y. 10118

612 Welland Avenue
St. Catharines
Ontario, Canada
L2M 5V6

73 Lime Walk
Headington
Oxford OX3 7AD
United Kingdom

Cataloging in Publication Data
Kalman, Bobbie, 1947-
    Big cats

(Crabapples)
Includes index.

ISBN 0-86505-610-2 (library bound)   ISBN 0-86505-710-9 (pbk.)
Many aspects of big cats, including camouflage, feeding, breeding, and different species, are examined in this book.

1. Felidae - Juvenile literature. I. Everts, Tammy, 1970-   .
II. Title. III. Series: Kalman, Bobbie, 1947-   . Crabapples.

QL737.C23K34 1994   j599.74/428 20   LC 94-5312
                                                           CIP

What is in this book?

Big cats

Some cats are little. Some cats are big. Big cats are not just bigger and heavier than little cats. They are different in other ways, too. Some little cats are wild, and others are pets. All big cats are wild. This jaguar would not make a good pet! Little cats meow, but most big cats **rrroarrr!**

A cat's body

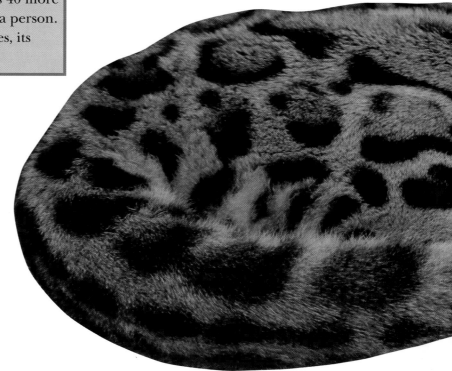

A cat's skeleton has 40 more bones than that of a person. When the cat relaxes, its body seems floppy.

Cats that live in hot places have short, thick fur. The fur keeps heat away from their bodies.

Cats have five toes on each foot, but they quietly tiptoe up to their prey on four toes.

Cats cannot sweat. They let off extra body heat through their feet.

A cat's tongue is covered with small spikes that scoop up liquid. A cat also uses its tongue for washing its fur.

Cats tear their food with their pointed teeth. They have no flat teeth, or **molars**, for chewing.

A cat's large ears help it hear even the quietest sounds.

A cat uses its whiskers the way you use your fingers to tell if an object is nearby.

Cats use their sense of smell more than any other sense. A tough pink pad protects the cat's delicate nose.

When a cat is not using its sharp claws for climbing or scratching, it pulls them into pockets in its paws.

Cats can see well at night. The black slits in a cat's eyes, called **pupils**, widen to let in more light.

A cat's eyes seem to glow in the dark. A layer in their eyes, called the **tapetum**, reflects light like a mirror.

Where do big cats live?

Big cats need big spaces to live.
Some big cats live in thick forests.
Some big cats live on snowy mountains.
Some big cats live on grassy plains.
Big cats live in trees, caves, and dens.
They do not like to live near people.

What's for dinner?

Big cats are **carnivores**. A carnivore is an animal that eats only meat. Big cats eat a huge amount of meat, but they do not always eat every day. Some big cats hunt in the evening. The cheetah prefers to hunt during the day.

Big cats eat small animals such as birds and mice and large animals such as zebras. Lions, leopards, and cheetahs sometimes fight one another for food.

Most cats hunt alone, but female lions hunt in groups. When an animal is killed, the male lions eat before the female lions do. The baby cats eat last.

Spots and stripes

Cheetahs, jaguars, and leopards all have spots. Look at the spots on the right. Using these as a guide, can you identify the spotted cat on the opposite page?

If you looked at different leopards, jaguars, or cheetahs, you would notice that each one has its own spot pattern. Even the stripes of tigers differ.

A cat's spot or stripe pattern is like a person's fingerprint. No two patterns are alike, just as no two people have the same fingerprints. Did you guess that the cat on page 12 is a leopard?

jaguar

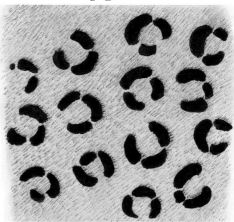

leopard

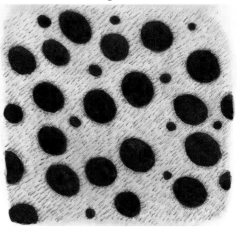

cheetah

Cats are mammals

Cats are **mammals**. Mammals have backbones and hair or fur. Mammals are **warm blooded**. Their body temperature stays the same no matter how warm or cold the weather is.

A female mammal carries her babies inside her body until they are born. Her newborn babies feed on her milk. Mammal mothers care for their young until the babies can look after themselves. Baby cats stay with their mother for several years.

Baby cats

Big cats can have one, two, three, or even four cubs at a time! Cubs are born blind. Their eyes open one or two weeks after they are born. Cubs are born without teeth. They get their baby teeth, or **milk teeth**, when they are several weeks old.

A cub squeaks and mews when it wants attention from its mother. The mother cat feeds and protects her babies. She teaches them to hunt and avoid enemies. Most father cats leave before the babies are born.

The cat family tree

The cat family tree is divided into big cats and little cats. Not all cats fit into these groups. The cheetah is in a family of its own, close to the big cats. The cougar is in its own family, close to the little cats. There are only four kinds of big cats, but there are many kinds of little cats. We could not show them all.

Big Cats

lion

leopard

jaguar

tiger

Cheetah

The **miacid** was a small carnivore that lived 40 million years ago. It is the ancestor of modern meat-eating animals such as cats, dogs, and bears.

Cougar

Little Cats

Pet cats

Wild cats

jaguarundi

margay

ocelot

manul

lynx

bobcat caracal

wildcat

fishing cat

serval

King of the Beasts

The lion is a big cat with a loud roar. It is sometimes called the King of the Beasts. Lions live on grassy plains called **savannahs**. They are the only cats that live in large families. A lion family is called a **pride**.

A female lion is called a **lioness**. She is smaller than a male lion. Lionesses take care of the cubs and do most of the hunting.

The male lion's job is to guard the pride. The big shaggy **mane** of fur around his neck makes him look big and fierce. It protects his head when he fights other male lions. Lionesses do not have manes.

 # Tiger tiger!

The tiger is the largest cat in the world. It can swim and climb trees. It is an excellent hunter. It hunts deer, wild pigs, and cows at night. Tigers live on grassy plains, in swamps, and in forests.

There are several kinds of tigers. They can be orange, yellow, or white, but they all have stripes. The white tiger on the left is a Bengal tiger. Its stripes are very pale.

Most tigers live where it is hot, but
the Siberian tiger prefers cold, snowy
forests. Siberian tigers are larger than
other tigers. There are fewer than 200
of these beautiful cats left in the wild.

Leopards

Most leopards live in thick rain forests. They live and hunt alone. A leopard sometimes hunts by sitting in a tree until an animal passes by. Then it pounces. Leopards often drag their meal up into a tree and eat it later.

Leopards can be different in size and color. The clouded leopard has splotches, stripes, and spots.

The snow leopard is rare. It lives in snowy mountain areas. It has beautiful spotted white fur.

The black leopard's spots are on top of its black fur. It is difficult to see them, but they are there! The black leopard is also called a **panther**.

clouded leopard

snow leopard

black leopard

The jaguar

The jaguar looks like a leopard, but it is larger and heavier. Its spots are bigger than those of the leopard. The two cats live in different parts of the world.

Jaguars live in hot places. They like swamps and forests. They hunt birds, fish, and deer at night. The jaguar also eats turtles and frogs. It swims well and is very good at catching fish.

 # The speedy cheetah

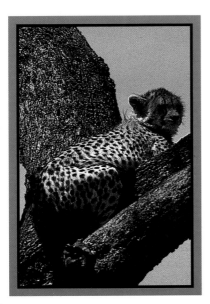

The cheetah is the fastest land animal in the world. It can run as fast as a car! Cheetahs are special cats that are neither big nor small. The cheetah is smaller and thinner than the big cats, but its legs are much longer. It cannot roar or pull in its claws. Cheetahs are not good at climbing trees, as other cats are. They can jump up into a tree, but they have a difficult time getting back down!

The cheetah lives on the savannah. It
can have up to five babies. Sometimes a
mother cheetah takes her babies hunting
with her, but the cubs are not very helpful.
They would rather play than hunt. They
are noisy and often scare away the prey.

Cats in danger

Big cats need to live and hunt in big spaces, but there are not many big, wild spaces left. As more people are born, they build more homes and use more land for growing food.

All big cats are **endangered**. They may soon be gone from the wild. Many cats starve to death because they have no place to hunt. Some people kill big cats for their beautiful fur.

Many people want to save wild cats before they are all gone. They are setting aside large areas, called **reserves**, where big cats and other animals will be safe. Governments have also passed laws to stop people from hunting endangered animals.

Words to know

ancestor Something from which something or someone is descended

carnivore An animal that eats only meat

endangered Describing an animal or plant that is in danger of dying out

mammal A class of warm-blooded animals with backbones and fur or hair

milk teeth The first teeth of a mammal

plain An area of level land

prey An animal hunted by another animal for food

pride A family or group of lions

reserve A huge park set aside for endangered animals

savannah A large, grassy plain

tapetum A layer in a cat's eyes that reflects light

warm-blooded Describing an animal whose body temperature is constant

Index

What is in the picture?

Here is some more information about the photographs in this book.

page:

cover	Leopards can be found in Africa and parts of Asia.
title page	Tigers live throughout India and other parts of Asia.
4-5	Jaguars live in the thick rain forests of Central and South America.
6-7	The rare clouded leopard makes its home in the forests of Asia.
6 (bottom)	A jaguar's long, sharp front teeth are perfect for tearing flesh from its prey.
7 (bottom)	The clouded leopard, like many cats, hunts at night.
8	A leopard naps in a tree. Cats sleep up to 18 hours a day.
9	Siberian tigers, like all cats, need plenty of rest.
10	Cheetahs live in Africa and parts of southern Asia.
11	Lion cubs are the last members of the pride to eat.
12	The white parts of a leopard's coat imitate the bits of light that shine through trees in the forest.
13	A tiger's stripes help it hide among tall grasses.
14-15	Lion cubs drink milk from their mother until they are three months old.
16-17	Sumatran tigers, like all baby big cats, are born with blue eyes.

page:

17	Cheetah cubs have spiky fur on their backs and necks. The fur gets smooth when they get older.
20	Lions sleep during the heat of the day and are active at night.
21	In each pride, there is one full-grown male but many females.
22 (top)	Bengal tigers live in the wetlands, plains, and forests of southern Asia.
22 (bottom)	White Bengal tigers are very rare.
23	Siberian tigers live in northern Asia. They are the largest of all big cats.
24	This leopard lives in the Masai Mara Reserve in Kenya.
25 (top)	Clouded leopards are endangered.
25 (bottom left)	Snow leopards live in northern Asia. They are very rare.
25 (bottom right)	Black leopards have been hunted for their beautiful and unusual coats. Today they are protected.
26	Jaguars are the only big cats that live in South America.
28 (top)	After running at top speed, cheetahs are so exhausted that they need to rest.
28 (bottom)	Cheetahs live on the savannahs of Africa.
29	This picture shows a mother cheetah watching over her cubs.
30	Mother cheetah keeps an eye out for her family's next meal.

5 6 7 8 9 0 Printed in USA 3 2 1 0